I0797325

Waves: Light and Sound

How Sound Changes

Robin Johnson and Douglas Hicton

LIGHTBOX
openlightbox.com

LIGHTBOX

Go to **www.openlightbox.com** and enter this book's unique code.

ACCESS CODE

LBXM9236

Lightbox is an all-inclusive digital solution for the teaching and learning of curriculum topics in an original, groundbreaking way. Lightbox is based on National Curriculum Standards.

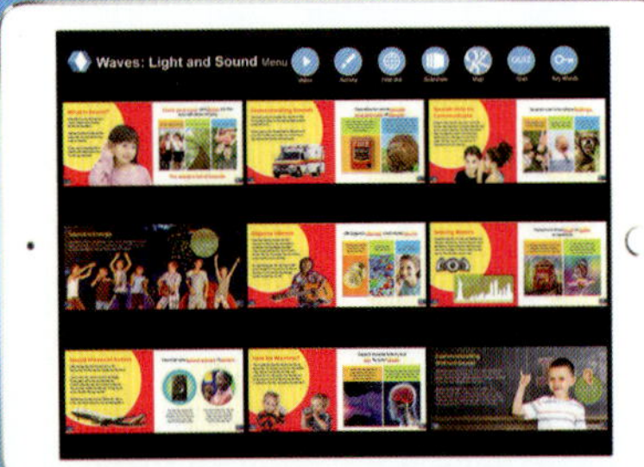

OPTIMIZED FOR

- ✓ TABLETS
- ✓ WHITEBOARDS
- ✓ COMPUTERS
- ✓ AND MUCH MORE!

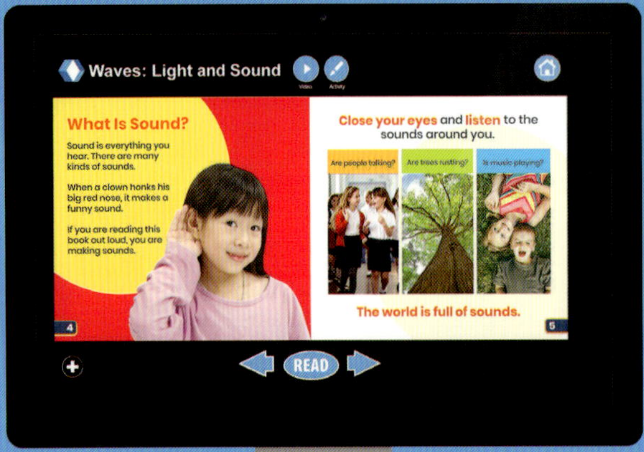

STANDARD FEATURES OF LIGHTBOX

 **AUDIO** High-quality narration using text-to-speech system

 **VIDEOS** Embedded high-definition video clips

 **ACTIVITIES** Printable PDFs that can be emailed and graded

 **WEBLINKS** Curated links to external, child-safe resources

 **SLIDESHOWS** Pictorial overviews of key concepts

 **INTERACTIVE MAPS** Interactive maps and aerial satellite imagery

 **QUIZZES** Ten multiple choice questions that are automatically graded and emailed for teacher assessment

 **KEY WORDS** Matching key concepts to their definitions

VIDEOS

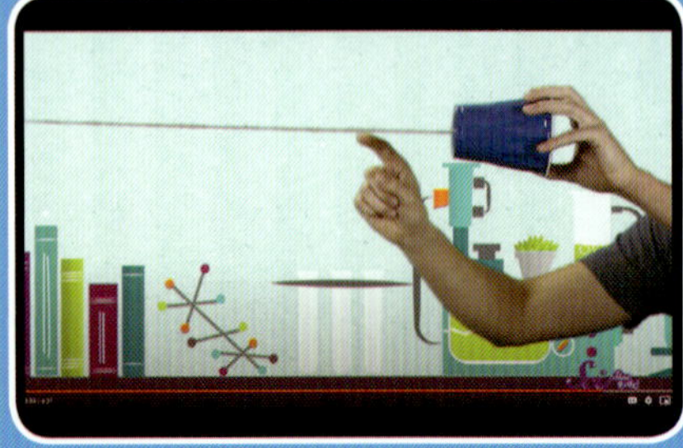

WEBLINKS

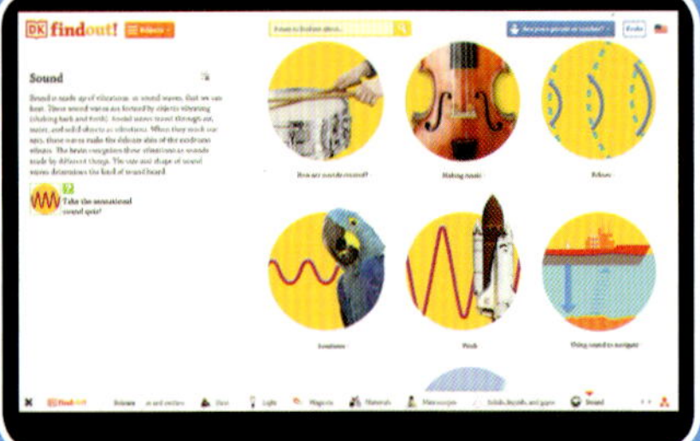

SLIDESHOWS

QUIZZES

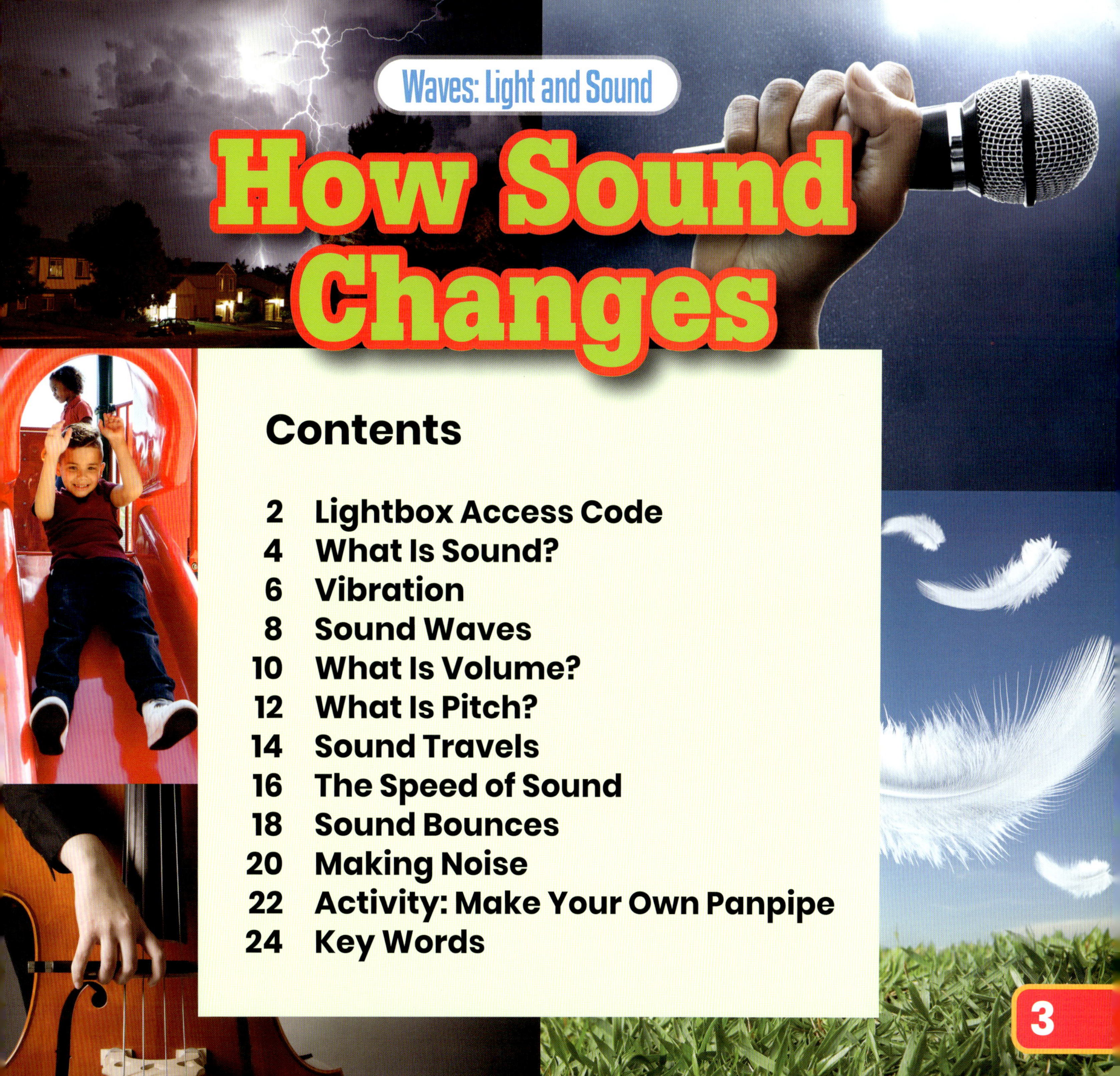

Waves: Light and Sound

How Sound Changes

Contents

What Is Sound?

Sound is all that you hear. People, animals, and objects make noises.

Your cat makes noise when it is hungry. Your alarm clock makes noise to get you out of bed. Your classroom can become very noisy, too!

Listen closely to the **sounds** around you.

Do you hear honking cars?

Do you hear mooing cows?

Do you hear laughing children?

Sounds can tell you where you are.

Vibration

A vibration is back and forth motion. Sound is a vibration. You can both hear and see it.

Stretch a rubber band between your fingers. Pluck it like a guitar string. You will see the rubber band vibrate. You will hear the sound it makes.

Small vibrations make **quiet** sounds.

A feather makes only a tiny vibration when it hits the ground. You cannot hear the sound without special tools.

Up close, a caterpillar eating a leaf makes a "Chomp! Chomp! Chomp!" sound.

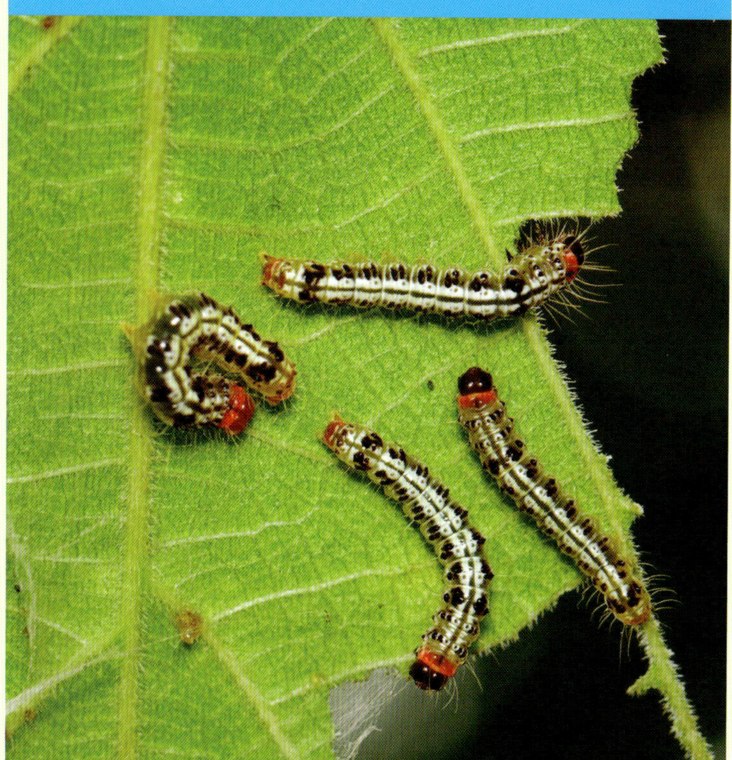

Sound Waves

Vibrating objects make sound waves. The waves travel to your ears. Your ears send them to your brain, which tells you what you are hearing.

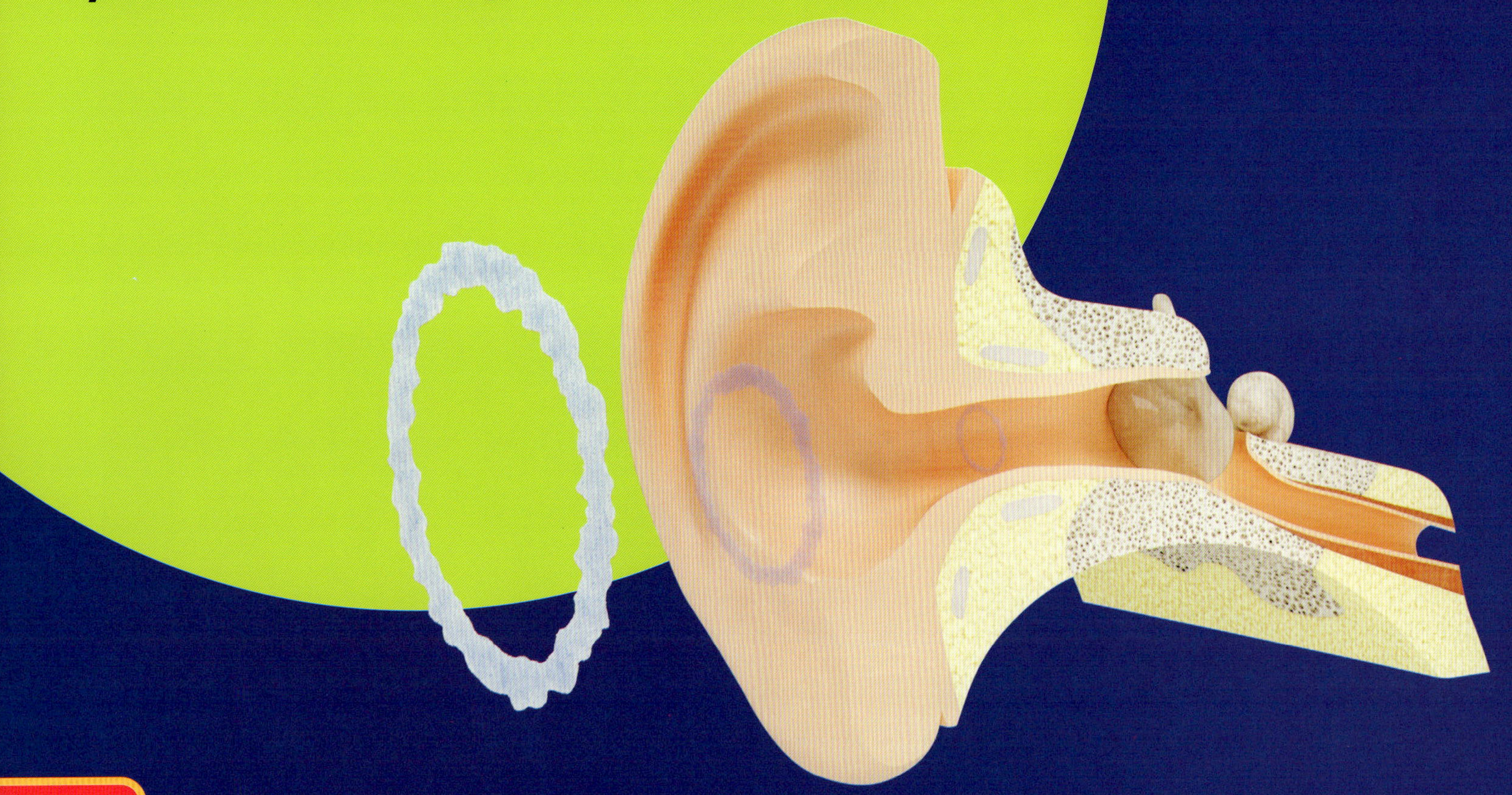

Loud sounds make **large sound waves**.

Airplanes make a loud "Boom!" sound.

Lions roar loudly to communicate.

Thunder makes a loud, rumbling noise.

What Is Volume?

Different sounds have different volumes. Volume is how loud or soft a sound is.

Some sounds are so loud that they can be dangerous. Harmful levels of noise are called noise pollution. Other sounds are so soft you can hardly hear them at all.

Music can be loud or soft. Listening to music at a high volume can harm your ears.

What Is Pitch?

Pitch is how high or low a sound is. Whistles and sirens are high sounds. Rolling thunder and foghorns are low sounds.

Fast vibrations are high-pitched. Slow vibrations are low-pitched. Pitch changes when vibrations change speed.

A **note** is a musical sound with a certain **pitch**.

A thin violin string vibrates quickly. It makes a high note.

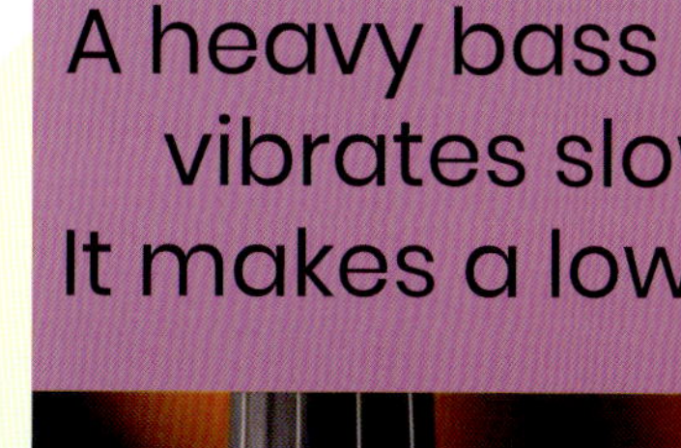

A heavy bass string vibrates slowly. It makes a low note.

Big instruments such as tubas play low notes.

Sound Travels

Sound waves travel through air and water. They also travel through solid materials such as wood and steel.

Sound waves need something to travel through. There is nothing for them to travel through in space. This means there is no sound in space.

Washington state's Mount St. Helens volcano erupted in 1980 with a blast that was heard hundreds of miles away.

Loud sounds **travel farther** than quiet sounds.

A rocket launching into space makes a very loud noise. Once the rocket is in space, however, it makes no sound.

Blue whales call to each other with loud sounds that can be heard from very far away.

The Speed of Sound

Sound waves move faster through water than through air. They move even faster through solid objects.

Whales live in the ocean. They communicate through the water. Some whales make noises that sound like songs. Other whales can hear them from very far away.

Sound can help you **understand** the world around you.

Sound can help you figure out how far you are from a thunderstorm. Count the seconds between lightning and thunder. Divide the number by 5. You are that many miles away.

You can listen through a wall. Place the top of a drinking glass against the wall. Put your ear against the bottom. The glass will make the sound louder.

Sound Bounces

Sound waves bounce off objects. Some sound waves return to the place where the sound began. Sound waves that bounce back are called echoes.

You can make an echo. Stand far away from a big wall or steep mountain. Shout and your words will come back to you!

Some **animals** use **echoes** to help them move around.

Bats make clicking sounds in the dark. The sounds echo off objects, guiding the bats safely around them.

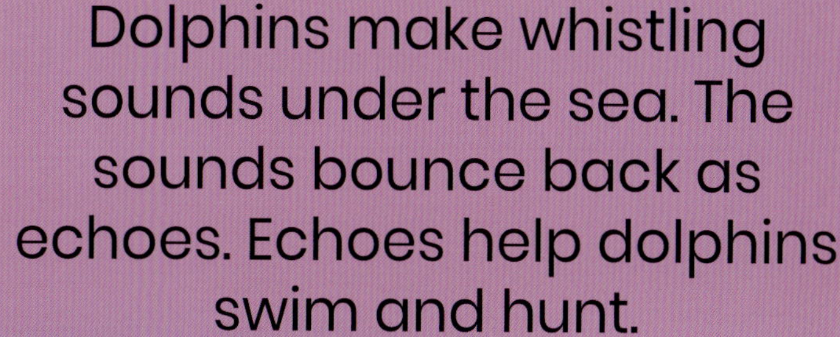

Dolphins make whistling sounds under the sea. The sounds bounce back as echoes. Echoes help dolphins swim and hunt.

Making Noise

We use our bodies to make sound. We clap our hands, snap our fingers, stamp our feet, and whistle. Mostly, we make sounds by talking.

Some people make a living with their voice. They may be singers or TV announcers. What are some other jobs where people use their voice?

Activity

Make Your Own Panpipe

A panpipe is a musical instrument made of tubes, or pipes. The pipes are of different lengths. They all play different notes. Each pipe has a column of air inside. The air vibrates when you blow into the pipe, making sound.

Supplies

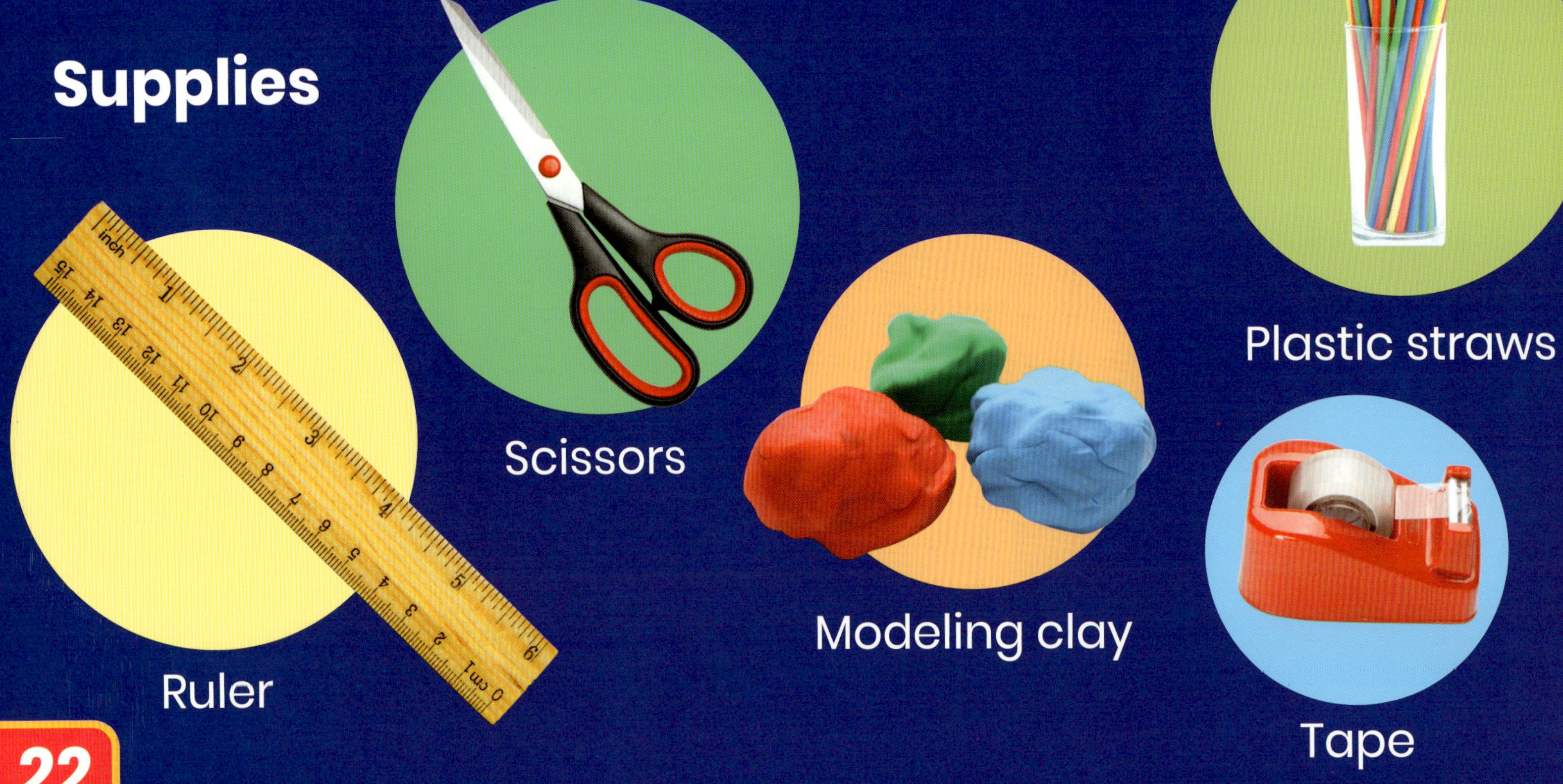

STEP 1 Cut each straw about half an inch shorter than the one before it.

STEP 2 Line up the straws, longest to shortest. Tape them together. The top edge should be even.

STEP 3 Plug the bottom of each straw with some clay.

STEP 4 Hold the pipes straight up and down in front of you with the open ends of the straws facing up. Blow gently across the open ends. Make music!

KEY WORDS

Research has shown that as much as 65 percent of all written material published in English is made up of 300 words. These 300 words cannot be taught using pictures or learned by sounding them out. They must be recognized by sight. This book contains 115 common sight words to help young readers improve their reading fluency and comprehension. This book also teaches young readers several important content words, such as proper nouns. These words are paired with pictures to aid in learning and improve understanding.

Page	Sight Words First Appearance
4	all, and, animals, can, get, hear, is, it, make, of, out, people, sound, that, to, too, very, what, when, you, your
5	are, around, cars, children, do, tell, the, where
6	a, back, between, both, like, see, will
7	close, only, small, up, without
8	them, which
9	large
10	about, Americans, at, be, different, from, have, high, how, or, other, so, some, they, work
12	changes
13	as, big, play, such, with
14	air, also, away, for, in, means, miles, need, no, something, state, there, this, through, was, water
15	call, each, far, into, once, than
16	even, live, move, songs
17	by, help, many, number, place, put, seconds, world
18	an, began, come, mountain, off, words
19	sea, under, use
20	feet, hands, may, on, our, their, we

Page	Content Words First Appearance
4	alarm clock, bed, cat, classroom, noises, objects
5	cows
6	fingers, guitar string, motion, rubber band, vibration
7	caterpillar, feather, ground, leaf, tools
8	brain, ears, sound waves
9	airplanes, lions, thunder
10	levels, music, noise pollution, volume
12	foghorns, pitch, sirens, speed, whistles
13	instruments, note, tubas
14	blast, materials, Mount St. Helens, space, steel, volcano, Washington, wood
15	blue whales, rocket
16	ocean
17	glass, lightning, thunderstorm, wall
18	echoes, mountain
19	bats, dolphins
20	bodies, decibels, jobs, power saw, scream, singers, TV announcers, voice

Published by Smartbook Media Inc.
14 Penn Plaza, 9th Floor New York, NY 10122
Website: www.openlightbox.com

Library of Congress Control Number: 2020937074

ISBN 978-1-5105-5399-6 (hardcover)
ISBN 978-1-5105-5400-9 (multi-user eBook)

Printed in Guangzhou, China
1 2 3 4 5 6 7 8 9 0 24 23 22 21 20

052020
110819

Project Coordinator: Priyanka Das
Designer: Jean Faye Marie Rodriguez

The publisher acknowledges Dreamstime, iStock, Minden, and Shutterstock as the primary image suppliers for this title.

First published by Crabtree Publishing Company in 2014.